The Little Book of
Plastic Lace Crafts

A Step-by-Step Guide to Making Lanyards, Key Chains, Bracelets, and other Crafts with Boondoggle, Scoubidou, Gimp, and Plastic Lace

Yonatan Setbon

BLOOM BOOKS
FOR YOUNG READERS

To my mom (Jessica Setbon) and to Dave Weeks (a.k.a. Boondoggleman),
the people behind my interest in lanyards.

Published by:
Bloom Books for Young Readers,
an imprint of Ulysses Press
PO Box 3440
Berkeley, CA 94703
www.ulyssespress.com

ISBN: 978-1-64604-501-3

Printed in China
10 9 8 7 6 5 4 3 2 1

Acquisitions editor: Casie Vogel
Project editor: Shelona Belfon
Managing editor: Claire Chun
Editor: Renee Rutledge
Proofreader: Barbara Schultz
Front cover design: Ashley Prine
Interior design and layout: Winnie Liu

Contents

Introduction

A Little Bit of History

No one really knows when the first lanyard was created. Lanyards are a subcategory of knots. Naturalists have recorded that orangutans make knots for pleasure. Perhaps an orangutan created a box stitch at one time in history. During the Great Depression, the jobless crafted lanyards as a form of make-work, and they used the word "boondoggle" for their creations. Lanyards were such a trend in the late 1920s that even the Prince of Wales (later Edward VIII) wore a boondoggle around his scout hat.

My Story

My personal journey with plastic lace crafts started when I was a child in 2003. I noticed my neighbor's unusual lanyard that alternated between a circle and a box. That lanyard made me realize that this craft had creative potential, and I was hooked immediately. I asked my mom to teach me the basic box stitch. It wasn't as easy as I thought it would be, but soon I started making basic shapes. After I exhausted what my mom had to teach me (not very much), we searched online and found boondoggleman.com, a website where Dave Weeks posted his work. After a few months, I learned everything I could from him as well, so I started inventing several new techniques, which I now share online. The process of developing these new methods greatly increased my confidence.

Then I moved on to making large sculptures—such as a snake, a bird, and the Eiffel Tower—from plastic lace. Each project involved at least a week of hard work. I contacted Boondoggleman and sent him photos of my sculptures. To my surprise, he replied and asked me if he could add them to his site. His recognition increased my motivation, and I set myself a goal of creating a dragon. I prepared for that by producing some introductory projects, such as a unicorn and a lion, which took two months. Then I asked, what's next?

By 2014, I had completed a chess set (that took nine months) and created my first human figure (a manga character called Naruto). That same year I launched my LanYarD YouTube channel by explaining how to create my dragon—that thirty-five-part tutorial took seventy-two hours of video and two full years to produce!

From 2014–2017, I explored the theoretical concepts of plastic lace craft, some mathematical theorems behind it, and some general concepts, such as the color combinations I discuss in Chapter 4. To me, considering the theoretical underpinnings of lanyards are no less important than creating them—I'm just as interested in understanding why I do this work as I am in creating something artistic.

In 2018–2019, I finished another manga figure (Itachi), a Pikachu, and Mega Lucario, one of my favorite Pokémon (which took me around thirteen months). I feel that my lanyards were less interesting in late 2019 and early 2020; perhaps the COVID-19 situation affected my creativity.

In January 2021, I jumpstarted my process by setting a theme for each year's work. While previously I aimed to create precise forms that matched clear visions of the final projects, in 2021 my goal was to use general knots, not just classic lanyard stitches. Over that year, instead of working on one project for months, I created four to five small projects each day. I compare this approach to the double pendulum motion (or butterfly effect) in mathematics: each small change can lead to a totally different and complex outcome. Because I was working on small projects, I was able to create more than a hundred items and to observe my style developing.

When January 2022 arrived, I made another change in artistic direction and decided to use cords without any knots. The project Knot-Free Lanyard—the first example in Chapter 7—is one such creation. Later in 2022, I searched for ways to incorporate simplicity into the complex designs of the previous year. Then I started testing a new technique: melting the plastic cords with an electric hot air gun (it doesn't burn the plastic). This changes the cord's shape and—together with the simplicity of working without knots—can lead to very interesting results.

After many years of being highly repetitive and exact and always using standard stitches in plastic lace crafts, I was inspired to break out and do something different. In some ways my recent works might be like Arnold Schoenberg's atonal compositions, which are ugly to some ears because they break the rules of tonality. To me, standard stitches are like classical tonality, and I wanted to break the monotony of using lanyards in a conventional way.

By not knowing what the outcome of a project will be, I rediscovered the adventure of creating something new and unexpected. The experience is like listening to a new piece of music or reading an unfamiliar story.

What's in This Book

Chapters 1–3 of this book show you how to make basic lanyard types in simple steps with easy explanations and diagrams for you to follow.

Chapter 4 describes color and structure combinations, the most basic of my theories of lanyards. I explain these in a very simple way, without any complicated math.

Chapters 5–6 contain more complicated stitches that are very popular on my LanYarD YouTube channel.

Chapter 7 introduces experimental processes for more adventuresome work.

Terminology

Lanyard: A lanyard typically consists of plastic lace material (cord) that is stitched or strung together. The definitions below will help acquaint you with the terminology used throughout this book.

Stitches: Stitches are what you normally use to create a lanyard. They can be defined as stacks of similar knots. There is the starting stitch, the first weave of a project, using some number of cords (could be even 1 cord). And there is a continuing stitch, which encompasses a whole part of a lanyard from one layer to the next one. For example, a box and a circle both start the same way, it is only after looking at a section of two close layers of the lanyard that you will be able to know if you did a box or a circle stitch.

Any stitch (both a starting stitch, and onward) can have two distinct presentations looking at it from above the lanyard. Usually these orientations–left hand or right hand–are mirror images of each other.

The instructions for a stitch I offer in the book use a sequence of three figures. The first figure is a layer with a specific size; it is the starting point of the stitch. The second figure is the process of how to continue to the next layer, using arrows to show what cord goes where, and which goes over, or under. The third figure is the layer of the result after stretching the cords if you follow the instructions of the second figure. Note that in the third image, the layer will always be realigned so that the warp and weft, or the two opposing cords, are horizontal and vertical to the page, similar to the alignment of the first figure. In reality, if the layer in the first figure stays fixed when creating the stitch, the next layer usually has an angle, because most stitches rotate.

Sometimes in the book I refer to the first figure and third figure as base, because these figures are also the result of the starting stitch. A base can be defined as the top layer. Any starting stitch is a base because the starting stitch has one layer by default. For any lanyard with two or more layers the base is as defined; it will be the top layer.

To summarize, a continuing stitch makes up the entire process from the first figure to the third figure. I could have given just the second figure and called it a day, but showing the first and third will show you aspects of orientation, if it were changed or kept the same, and sometimes in more complex stitches the color order of the cords might change. Showing only the second figure might be hard to some, and some of you might miss important details that accrue from one layer to the next.

Example of orientations and sizes:

| **1x1 left hand** | **1x1 right hand** | **2x1 left hand** | **2x1right hand** |

Here is an example of how to make a box stitch. The first figure is a 1x1 base showing that we have in the beginning a left-hand orientation, the second figure shows the arrows of how to get to the next layer. The third figure shows the result after stretching; as you can see it is now a right-hand orientation.

Not all stitches move you to a different orientation. A popular example of this is the circle stitch, whose arrows will send you back to the same orientation. Note that the third figure here is just a copy of the first; in reality the cords of the new layer would be pointed diagonally if the previous layer stayed still.

As previously stated, both stitches start with the same first figure. In other words, saying "how to start a box stitch" and saying "how to start a circle stitch" are the same, because they both start the same way. It is only the continuation that will be different.

Knots: The difference between a stitch and a knot is that a knot does not need to consist of layers. It can be a random tangle, like a knot that forms when you put your wired earphones in your pocket.

Cords: Cords are the plastic strands that are the main material for lanyards. While lanyards are typically made of knots or stitches, you can create interesting works without them.

Plastic: Plastic is the material that lanyard cord is made of. You can work with plastic in myriad ways. For instance, you can try melting the cords with an electric hot air gun, or taking small pieces of lanyard and using a plastic extruder to see what it does.

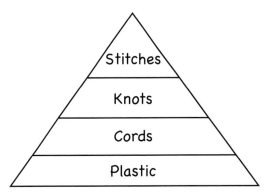

Over and under: This rule is used throughout the book, and it is extremely important to understand. When a cord crosses another cord twice, it should go over the closest cord and then go under the second. In example 1A (see steps 1A to 3A), see how the magenta cord on the left first goes over the white cord, then goes under it. This rule is fundamental, and if you ignore it, you won't get the result you want in most cases (everything will fall apart). Example 1B shows a cord on the right that needs to go over two pairs of cords—the black cord and the gray cord. It needs to go over and under twice, which means it starts over the black cord, then under the black cord, then over the gray cord, and finally under the gray cord.

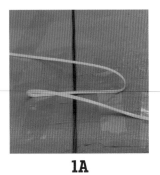
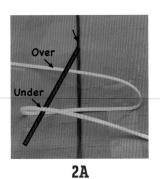
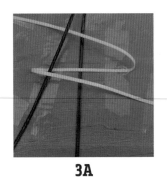
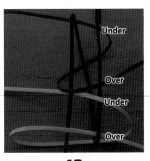

| 1A | 2A | 3A | 1B |

Orientation (right hand and left hand): Orientation is the position of the base, given the location of the loops and cords in relation to one another.

- Each border of a base consists of loops and ends of cords.
- Each loop is between two ends, and each end is between two loops.

There are always two possibilities of orientations for any given size of a base. Given any base, you can create a similar size base that is different from the original, by changing all loops to an end and vice versa. Meaning that if a point in the border of the original was an end, the same point on the new base will be a loop. If a point in the border of the original was a loop, the same point on the new base will be an end. Therefore the new base determines the orientation.

In this book, I use two possibilities of orientation: "left-hand orientation" and "right-hand orientation."

Left-hand orientation: On the side that is close to you, the end of the cord will be located on the far-left side.

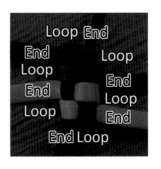
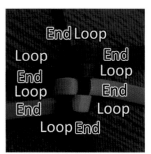

Right-hand orientation: On the side that is close to you, the end of the cord will be located on the far-right side.

Left-hand   Right-hand

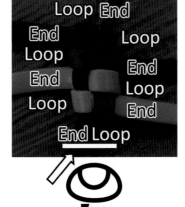

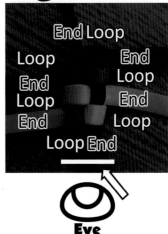

Eye   Eye

Stretching: Stretch is the default action you use to create a stitch. It takes some practice because it involves hand coordination. As an exercise before you stretch a lanyard, try stretching two overhand knots simultaneously. This might help you, because usually in making lanyards you will need to stretch at least two cords with one hand. An experienced maker can learn to control one cord with each finger, like a pianist pressing different keys with different forces.

Equipment: At the start of each project in this book, I list the specific materials you will need: general equipment, the kind and number of cords, and so on. Cords for making plastic lace crafts are available from Amazon, eBay, and craft stores. I personally use the brands Rexlace and Toner Crafts.

If you find it difficult to hold the cord, you can use tape to hold it in place, like I did in the examples pictured in Chapter 1.

If you find it hard to make an end stitch, you can use superglue to cement the end. Keep in mind that glue is very unpredictable and it can leave white stains on your stitch. So before using the glue, try testing it, and remember to never touch the glue while it is still wet.

I strongly suggest having fingernail scissors handy, not only for cutting cords but also to use as a needle, a way to help you with the weaving process.

Finally, bring any other equipment you want to add to your lanyard project. I sometimes attach lanyards to canvas paintings or combine lanyards with fishing cords and beautiful stone beads. You might also consider using rainbow looms, other kinds of cords such as macrame, organic materials, and possibly origami. Anything goes in plastic lace crafts, as long as it is creative.

Length of cords: Unless I indicate otherwise, the length of cords for the short lanyards in this book should be around three feet. If you're making a large stitch, then I suggest using around six to eight feet (two to three meters) maximum.

Chapter 1
Basic Starting Stitches

A basic stitch is formed by interlacing two sets of warp and weft. Note, in the explanations below, warp refers to the vertical cords and weft to the horizontal cords. This chapter introduces rectangular starting stitches.

As said in the introduction, the starting stitch for a box and for a circle is the starting stitch and it is the size of a 1x1, one cord on each side.

This goes as well for other sizes, in a 2x1 for example there are 6 different continuing (brick, twist, swirl, chevron, inverse-chevron, octagonal) stitches that can be done, and all of them start the same way that is presented here in this chapter.

In later chapters, you will see that your starting stitch does not have to be a rectangle or square. You can start with many different shapes, such as a triangle, pentagon, hexagon, or any polygon.

Starting a 1x1

- Scissors
- 2 (1-foot) strands of lanyard cord
- Scotch tape

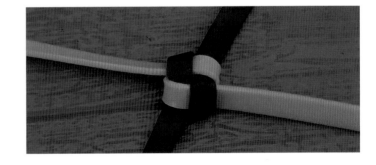

1. Start by cutting your weft to a 1-foot length. Measure the warp against the weft and cut it to equal size.

2. Position the 2 cords perpendicular to each other, with the center of the weft (white) cord crossing the center of the warp (red) cord. Tape both cords on each side, about an inch from where they intersect with each other.

3. Bring the left weft cord to the bottom right and the right weft cord to the top left.

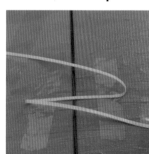

4. Fold the top of the warp cord down, crossing it over and under the weft.

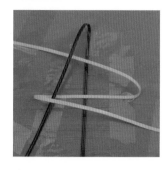

5. Fold the bottom of the warp cord up, crossing it over and under the weft.

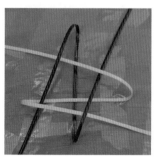

6. Remove the tape and stretch the ends of the four cords to make your left-hand box stitch.

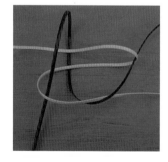

Starting a 2x1

The brick stitch is similar to the box stitch but has a 2x1 base.

- Scissors
- 2 (1-foot) strands of lanyard cord
- 1 (2-foot) strand of lanyard cord
- Scotch tape

The Little Book of Plastic Lace Crafts

1. Start by cutting 2 weft cords to 1-foot lengths. Measure the warp against the weft and cut it to twice the size.

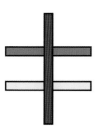 

2. Position 2 weft (brown and yellow) cords parallel to one another and the warp (red) cord over the center of them. Tape the warp cord about an inch above where it intersects the top weft cord and an inch below where it intersects the bottom weft cord.

 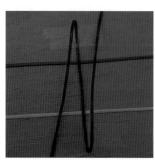

3. Fold the top of the warp cord down to the bottom left and the bottom of the warp cord up to the top right.

 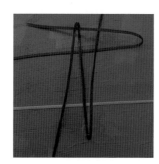

4. Starting with the top weft (brown) cord, fold the right side to the left, over and under the warp cord.

 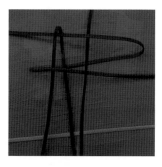

5. Next, fold the same weft cord to the right, over and under the warp cord.

 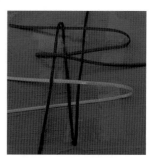

6. Repeat with the bottom weft (yellow) cord.

 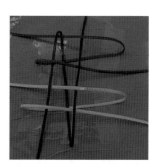

7. Remove the tape and stretch the ends of the six cords to make your left-hand brick stitch.

Chapter 2

Building from the Basic Stitches

Now that you've got the hang of the basic stitches, it's time for the real fun to begin. This chapter will show you how to extend a variety of stitches to create lanyards of many shapes and sizes.

Continuing a 1x1: Box Stitch

- Scissors
- 2 (1.5-foot) strands of lanyard cord
- Scotch tape

1. Create a left-hand box stitch base, following steps 1–6 that start on page 11.

2. Fold the top warp cord down to the bottom right and the bottom warp cord up to the top left.

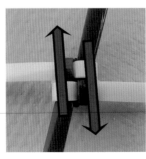

3. Then weave the 2 weft cords over and under the warp cords.

 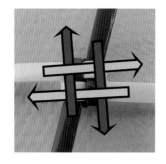

4. Stretch to tighten. Note that your left-hand box stitch is now a right-hand box stitch.

5. Repeat steps 2–4, but with the warp cords and the weft cords in mirror image to their previous positions.

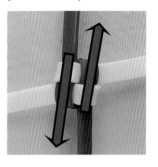 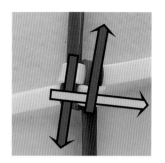

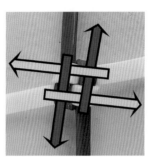

6. Repeat steps 1–5 to create additional box stitches.

Continuing a 1x1: Circle Stitch

The circle stitch is the second way to continue a 1x1 box stitch.

- Scissors
- 2 (1.5-foot) strands of lanyard cord
- Scotch tape

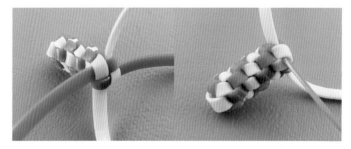

1. Create a left-hand box stitch base, following steps 1–6 on page 11.

2. Fold the top warp cord down diagonally to the bottom left and the bottom warp cord up diagonally to the top right.

3. Weave the weft cords over and under the warp cords diagonally. Stretch to tighten. Note that your left-hand box stitch remains a left-hand box stitch throughout the weaving.

4. Repeat steps 1–3 to create additional circle stitches.

Continuing a 2x1: Brick Stitch

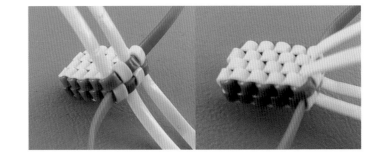

- Scissors
- 2 (3-foot) strands of lanyard cord
- 1 (1.5-foot) strand of lanyard cord
- Scotch tape

1. Create a left-hand brick stitch base, following steps 1–7 on page 12.

2. Fold the top warp cord down to the bottom right and the bottom warp cord up to the top left.

3. Weave each weft cord, in order from top to bottom, over and under the warp cords. Stretch to tighten. Note that your left-hand brick stitch is now a right-hand brick stitch.

  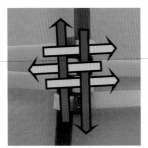 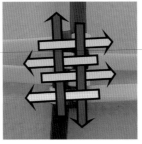 

4. Repeat steps 2–3, but with the warp cords and the weft cords mirror images from their previous positions.

 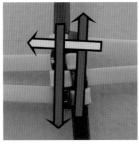 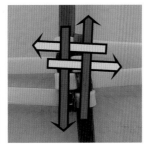 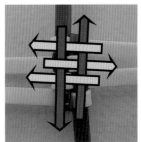 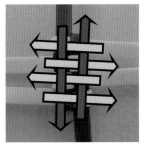

5. Repeat steps 1–4 to create additional brick stitches.

Continuing a 2x1: Twist Stitch

The twist stitch is similar to the circle stitch but has a 2x1 base.

- Scissors
- 2 (3-foot) strands of lanyard cord
- 1 (1.5-foot) strand of lanyard cord
- Scotch tape

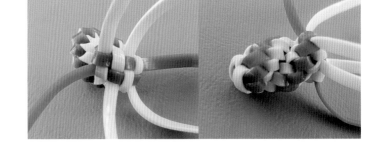

1. Create a left-hand brick stitch base, following steps 1–7 on page 12.

2. Fold the top warp cord down diagonally to the bottom left and the bottom warp cord up diagonally to the top right.

3. Weave each weft cord, in order from top to bottom, over and under the warp cords. Stretch to tighten. Note that your left-hand

twist stitch remains a left-hand twist stitch throughout the weaving.

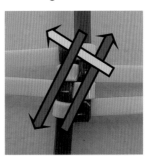 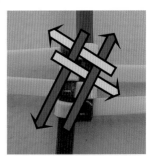

4. Repeat steps 2–3 to create additional twist stitches.

Chapter 3

End Stitches

An end stitch is a way to finish a stitch so that it won't come apart. Creating an end stitch is the best way to complete a project. An alternative is to glue or melt the plastic lace with a soldering heat gun.

The end stitch is generally the same for each lanyard. However, in Chapter 7, I'll discuss modern approaches where the end stitches give interesting and unusual shapes to what it seems, at first, are ordinary lanyards.

Note, in this chapter I numbered the cords in the figures to help explain the instructions.

Ending a 1x1: Box Stitch

1. Weave a 1x1 left-hand stitch (page 11), but do not stretch it.

2. Run cord 1 under cord 2, then pull it through the center of the loop.

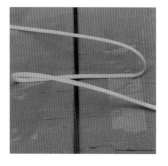 

3. Run cord 2 under cord 3, then pull it through the center of the loop.

4. Run cord 3 under cord 4, then pull it through the center of the loop.

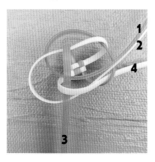

5. Finally, run cord 4 under cord 1, then pull it through the center of the loop.

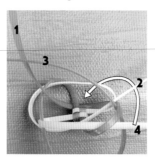 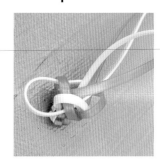

6. Stretch the stitch to tighten. Cut excess cord, no closer than your width of you thumb from the knot.

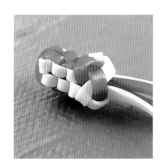

Ending a 2x1: Brick Stitch

1. Weave a 2x1 left-hand stitch (page 12), but do not stretch it.

2. Run cord 1 around and between cord 2 and 6 under 4, and then pull it through the center of the loops.

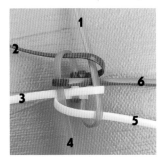
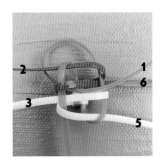

3. Run cord 2 around and between cord 3 and 6 under 4, and then pull it through the center of the loops.

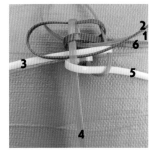

4. Continue running the remaining four cords around the closest cord, then through the center: cord 4 between cords 1 and 5, then 5 between 3 and 6 (and under 1), and finally 6 between 1 and 2.

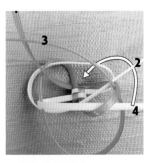
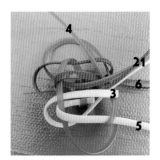

5. Stretch the cords by pulling all six ends. First pull all cords at the same time, then pull each cord individually until all ends are tight. Cut excess cord, no closer than your width of you thumb from the knot.

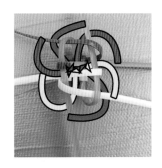

Chapter 4

Playing with Color and Structure

So far in this book, I've covered the basics for starting, continuing, and ending traditional lanyards. In this chapter, I will build on that and offer some variations in color and structure that use the basic techniques. By switching your cord colors and using squared stitches, round stitches, or a combination of both, you can make lanyards with countless designs. Here are some examples for 1x1:

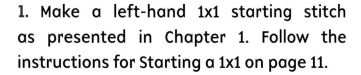

Square Lanyard

A square lanyard consists of only box stitches. In this project I've used two colors.

- Scissors
- 2 (1-foot) strands of lanyard cord
- Scotch tape

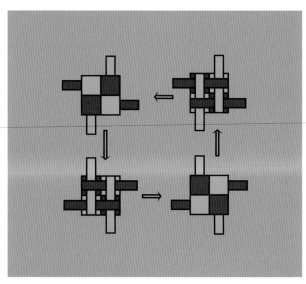

1. Make a left-hand 1x1 starting stitch as presented in Chapter 1. Follow the instructions for Starting a 1x1 on page 11.

2. Continue the box stitch. Follow the instructions for Continuing a 1x1: Box Stitch on page 14.

3. Complete the lanyard. Follow the instructions for Ending a 1x1: Box Stitch on page 18.

Switching Lanyard Version 1

This lanyard rotates in one direction and then switches and rotates in the other direction. For the first half of this project, you will create right-hand circle stitches, then create a box stitch. Then you will continue with left-hand circle stitches.

- Scissors
- 2 (1.5-foot) strands of lanyard cord
- Scotch tape

1. Make a left-hand 1x1 starting stitch as presented in Chapter 1. Follow the instructions for Continuing a 1x1: Circle Stitch on page 15. Repeat for 10 to 15 stitches. Note that your stitches will be left-hand stitches.

2. Create 1 box stitch. Now you will have a right-hand base.

3. Create 10 to 15 circle stitches by following the instructions for Continuing a 1x1: Circle Stitch but in mirror image.

4. Create an end stitch. Follow the instructions for Ending a 1x1: Box Stitch on page 18.

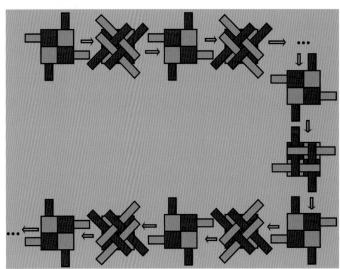

Standard Twist Lanyard

A standard twist starts the same way as the 2x1 starting stitch covered in Chapter 1. It uses three cords; to show them clearly I used three different colors.

- Scissors
- 2 (2-foot) strands of lanyard cord
- 1 (4-foot) strand of lanyard cord
- Scotch tape

1. Make a left-hand brick stitch base. Follow the instructions for Starting a 2x1 on page 12. In the example the 2 vertical cords were red and bright yellow, and the horizontal cord was mustard yellow.

2. Continue the stitch. Follow the instructions for Continuing a 2x1: Twist Stitch on page 17.

3. Complete the lanyard. Follow the instructions for Ending a 2x1: Brick Stitch on page 19.

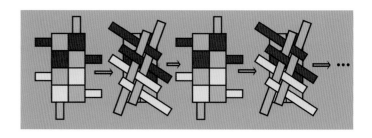

Switching Lanyard Version 2

Similar to the Switching Lanyard Version 1 on page 21, this project uses a 2x1 base rather than a 1x1 base. It rotates in one direction and then switches and rotates in the other direction. For the first half of this project, you will create right-hand circle stitches, then create a brick stitch. Then you will continue with left-hand circle stitches.

- Scissors
- 2 (2-foot) strands of lanyard cord
- 1 (4-foot) strand of lanyard cord
- Scotch tape

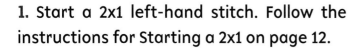

1. Start a 2x1 left-hand stitch. Follow the instructions for Starting a 2x1 on page 12.

2. Continue the stitch. Follow the instructions for Continuing a 2x1: Twist Stitch on page 17. Create ten to fifteen stitches.

3. Create 1 brick stitch. Follow the instructions for Continuing a 2x1: Brick Stitch on page 16.

4. Continue with 10 to 15 twist stitches. Follow the instructions for Continuing a 2x1: Twist Stitch on page 17.

5. Complete the lanyard. Follow the instructions for Ending a 2x1: Brick Stitch on page 19.

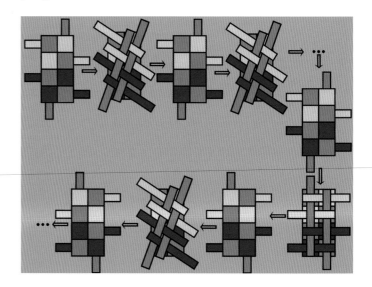

Chapter 5

Larger Stitches

In this chapter, I'll give some practical instructions for a larger 5x1 stitch.

5x1: Twist-Swirl Stitch

This project uses two alternating stitches. The pattern consists of twist, swirl, twist, swirl, etc. It can be done from sizes 2x1 onward. The result is a flat lanyard with a pattern of colors on the surface that seems random at first glance. In this example I will show how it's done with a size 5x1 to show you the general idea, and the stitch will be large enough for you to understand how to do it in larger or smaller scale using stitches that start with one cord at one side, such as 2x1, 4x1, 8x1, etc.

- Scissors
- 6 (7-foot) strands of lanyard cord

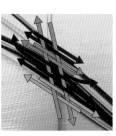

1–4. Tie 6 overhand knots on a cord. The sides of the overhand knots are the weft cords, and the cord that they are attached to is the warp cord (here the tan cord).

5–6. Create a 5x1 stitch. The arrows show how to create it. Start with the horizontal cords (here they are gold). The vertical cords go over and under, starting with the top red cord. The final cord will be the bottom turquoise.

| 1 | 2 | 3 | 4 | 5 | 6 |

7–10. Create a twist stitch by looping the bottom cord up to the left side and the top cord down to the right side. Then weave the weft cords over and under the warp cords in order.

11–14. After finishing the twist stitch, create a swirl by folding the left cord up on the left side and the right cord down on the right side. Then weave the weft cords in order.

15–26. Repeat steps 7–12 numerous times.

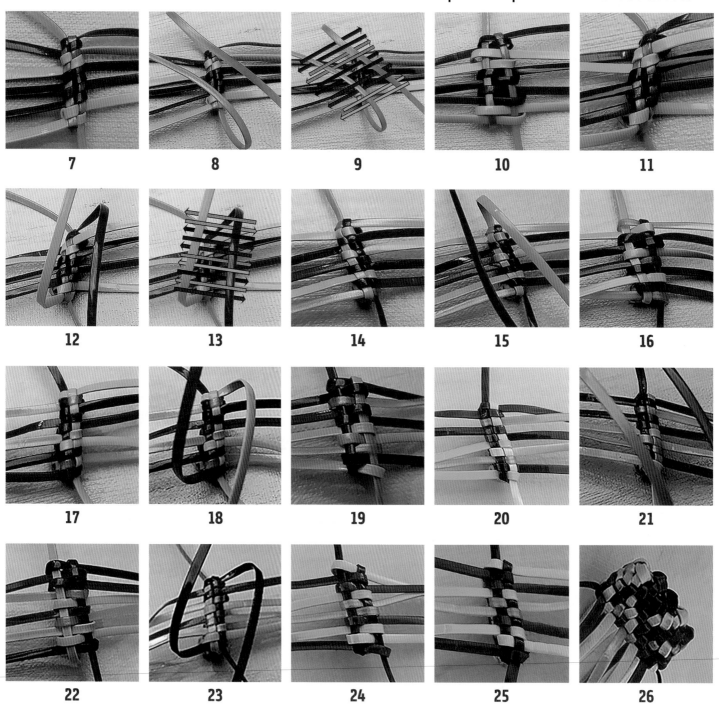

7

8

9

10

11

12

13

14

15

16

17

18

19

20

21

22

23

24

25

26

The Little Book of Plastic Lace Crafts

27–29. After creating around 15 stitches, make one 5x1 brick stitch. This will make the pattern a bit more interesting, because now you will start to get a different pattern.

30–44. After that brick stitch, continue with a swirl, then twist, swirl, etc.

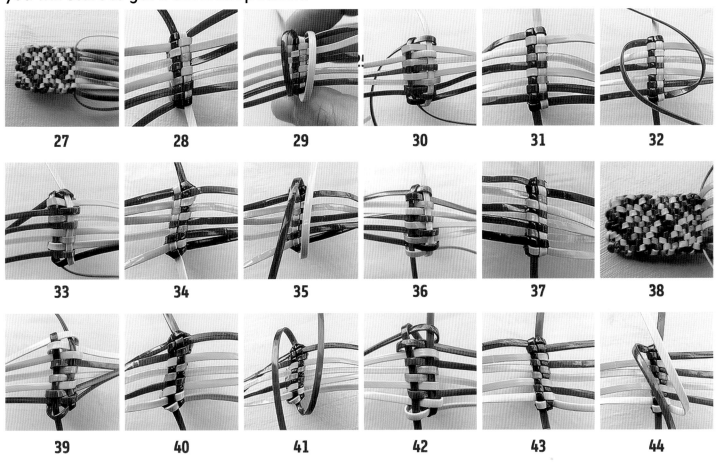

45–53. To finish the lanyard, create 3 4-cord box stitches and finish each with an end stitch.

Chapter 6

Recentered Stitches

This chapter returns to the basic box and circle stitches but extends them in such a way that their behavior changes completely. I got this idea back in 2021, when I started moving one strand to the center of each box (or circle) stitch. I call this type of stitch a recentered stitch. This minor change can lead to very unexpected results and endless new lanyards that are based on the boxes and circles.

Natural Recentered Stitches

Creating one natural recentered box stitch causes the overall shape to bend in an angle not perpendicular to the surface of the stitch. Doing this multiple times using the same cord to recenter will curl the lanyard like a leg of a squid and, in the end, it can take on the shape of a seashell.

- Scissors
- 2 (5-foot) strands of lanyard cord
- Scotch tape

1. Make a left-hand box stitch base. Follow the instructions for Starting a 1x1 on page 11, but do not stretch the stitch.

2–3. Take one cord and pull it clockwise through the center of the stitch in the same way you would make an end stitch.

4. Make another box stitch, but do not stretch the stitch.

5–6. Take the same cord as in steps 2–3 and pull it clockwise through the center of the stitch in the same way you would make an end stitch.

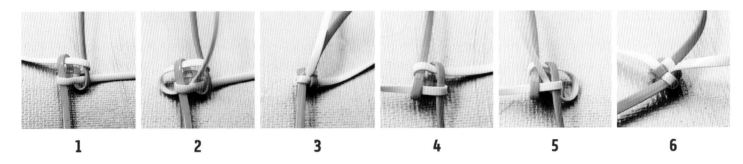

| 1 | 2 | 3 | 4 | 5 | 6 |

7. Repeat steps 2–6, always using the same cord.

If you use a circle stitch instead of a box stitch, you will get the shape shown in figure 6 below.

1. Make a left-hand circle stitch. Follow the instructions for Continuing a 1x1: Circle Stitch on page 15, but do not stretch the stitch.

2–3. Take 1 cord and pull it clockwise through the center of the stitch in the same way you would make an end stitch.

4–5. Make another circle stitch, but do not stretch the stitch. Take the same cord as in steps 2–3 and pull it clockwise through the center of the stitch in the same way you would make an end stitch.**6.** Repeat steps 2–5, while always using the same cord. The lanyard will not curl in on itself, like the natural recentered box stitch does.

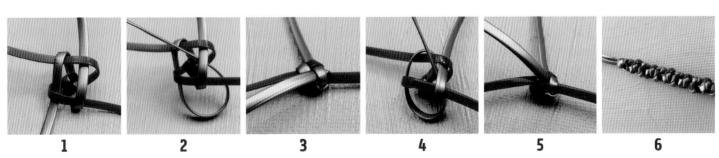

| 1 | 2 | 3 | 4 | 5 | 6 |

Unnatural Recentered Stitches

To make unnatural recentered stitches, rotate the cord through the center in a direction opposite that of natural recentered stitches. If you're working on a left-hand stitch, rotate counterclockwise (and clockwise on a right-hand stitch). This stitch gives the box stitch a totally different result.

- Scissors
- 2 (5-foot) strands of lanyard cord
- Scotch tape

1. Make a left-hand box stitch base. Follow the instructions for Starting a 1x1 on page 11. Fold the cords to make the next box stitch, but do not tighten them.

2. Take 1 cord and pull it counterclockwise through the center of the stitch in the same way you would make an end stitch.

3. Stretch the stitch tight.

4–5. Make another box stitch, but do not stretch the stitch. Take the same cord as in steps 2–3 and pull it counterclockwise through the center of the stitch in the same way you would make an end stitch.

6. Repeat steps 2–5, while always using the same cord.

| 1 | 2 | 3 | 4 | 5 | 6 |

An unnatural recentered stitch made with a circle stitch will make the shape of a Moroccan tea cookie.

1. Make a left-hand circle stitch. Follow the instructions for Continuing a 1x1: Circle Stitch on page 15. Make another circle stitch, but do not stretch it.

2–3. Take one cord and pull it counterclockwise through the center of the stitch in the same way you would make an end stitch.

4–5. Make another circle stitch, but do not stretch the stitch. Take the same cord as in steps 2–3 and pull it counterclockwise through the center of the stitch in the same way you would make an end stitch.

6. Repeat steps 2–5, while always using the same cord.

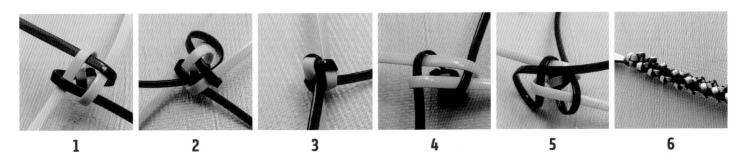

Extended Stitch

Recentered stitches are a type of extended stitch. An extended 1x1 stitch starts with either a box stitch or a circle stitch. From there you can continue weaving the cords however you like to create new forms. You can move one, two, or more cords anywhere around or inside the stitch, as many times as you want to. By first creating a box stitch or a circle stitch, you will make sure that your stitch will not fall apart after stretching.

1. Make a left-hand box stitch base. Follow the instructions for Starting a 1x1 on page 11.

2. In this example of extending the box, you move one cord.

3. In this example, you move two cords.

| 1 | 2 | 3 |

While you can weave in any manner, if you repeat the same extended stitch throughout your project, the result will have a coherent structure. Therefore, I recommend using a natural recentered stitch or an unnatural recentered stitch, as these are the simplest (and at the same time most interesting) extended 1x1 stitches I know of.

Natural — Square — Circle   Unnatural — Square — Circle

The Little Book of Plastic Lace Crafts

Chapter 7

Creativity without Stitching

You can make creative lanyards without using stitches. The chapter is intended for readers who want to explore the possibilities of plastic lace crafts rather than follow standard designs for them. If you feel ready for something different but in the same spirit as the earlier exercises, here are three examples.

Knot-Free Lanyard

You can make this simple project by creating holes and not using a single knot.

- Scissors
- 2 (2-foot) strands of lanyard cords
- 1 (1-inch) strand of lanyard cord

1–2. Fold your main cord and then cut along the folded edge to make a small hole at the center. If you cut a larger hole, you can insert two or more cords through the hole. You can use two main cords, like the silver cords shown here, to make it more interesting insert one main cord in a hole in the other.

3. Insert another cord (here the yellow cord) through the hole.

4–5. Fold the new cord as you did the first, and cut a hole.

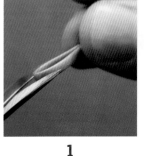

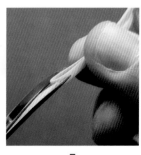

| 1 | 2 | 3 | 4 | 5 |

6. Insert the first cord through the second cord through the new hole to form a loop.

7. Add very short cords (the black cords in this example) to act like beads along the main cord. Cut a hole into the bead and slide it over the main cord.

8-9. Continue adding to the lanyard as you wish.

6

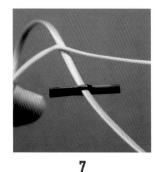

7

8

9

Cobra Stitch Lanyard

This project uses a stack of cords and a stitch called the cobra stitch.

- Scissors
- 1 (3-foot) strand of lanyard cord
- 3 (half-foot) strands of lanyard cord

1. Gather the 3 short cords.

2. Tie an overhand knot with the long cord around the 3 short cords. An overhand knot with one or more cords within it is called a cobra stitch.

3–4. Tie 4 to 5 additional cobra stitches to secure the three cords.

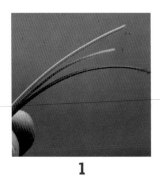

1

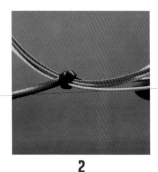

2

3

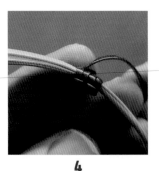

4

The Little Book of Plastic Lace Crafts

5–8. Make overhand knots with the long cord however you like. You can either add them between the cords or not. You can even create overhand knots with a single side of the cord, which is an example of a thing that is not a stitch.

9–10. Rejoin the two sides of the cord with an overhand knot.

11–12. Add a few more overhand knots after the rejoining.

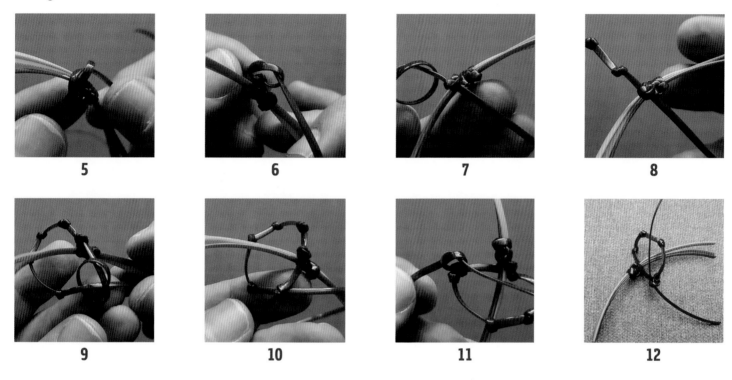

5	6
7	8
9	10
11	12

Rings of Saturn Lanyard

This project uses wound cords, overhand knots, and the cobra stitch. The white cord keeps the other cords intact.

- Scissors
- 3 (6-foot) strands of lanyard cord

1–3. Wind a cord into a circle 4 to 6 times.

4. With a second cord, create an overhand knot around the stack of cords. An overhand knot with one or more cords within it is called a cobra stitch.

5–6. Tie 4 to 5 additional cobra stitches to secure the circle.

7. Wind another circle with the second side of the first cord, in the opposite direction.

8–9. Use the cobra stitch to secure the second circle, then tie it to the first circle with an overhand knot.

10–11. Wind a third cord into a circle between the 2 previous circles. Wind this new circle fewer times (3 to 4 times).

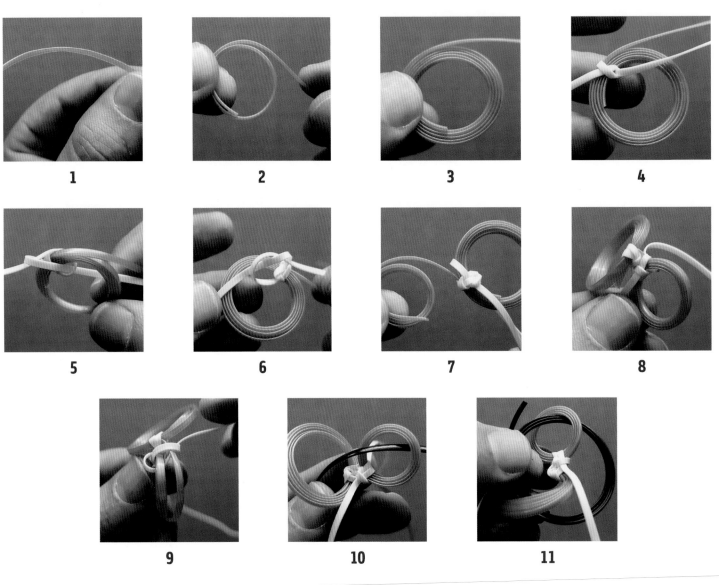

1

2

3

4

5

6

7

8

9

10

11

12–16. With the second cord, use the cobra stitch to secure the third circle. Then use overhand stitches to attach it to the first two circles. After the third circle is secured, you can add overhand knots however you like, either tying them onto one of the circles or without anything inside the knot.

17–19. To finish the project, create a stitch with the second cord and close the stitch after the first stitch.

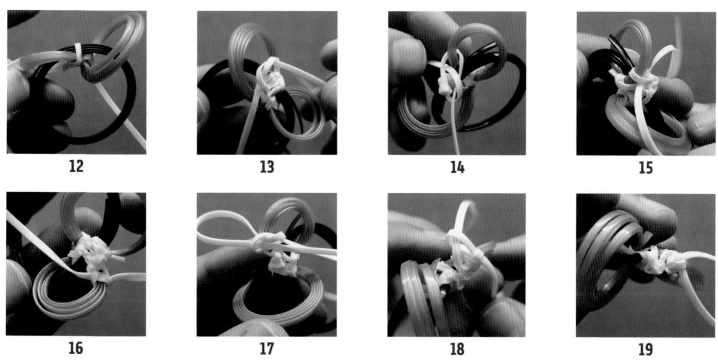

12

13

14

15

16

17

18

19

Conclusion

Making lanyards can be difficult, especially for beginners who have never completed a box stitch. It can be like your first experience tying your shoes. I hope this is just the start of your plastic lace crafts journey, and I hope you continue challenging yourself with the next new idea.

See you soon in the next book!

About the Author

For over eight years, Yonatan Setbon has maintained a YouTube channel dedicated to lanyards. After mastering the content available on the internet, he began to explore and develop his own new techniques, both practical and creative. In 2008, when Yonatan was sixteen, his art was showcased on the website of expert crafter Boondoggleman. On Yonatan's YouTube channel, you can find the basics, as well as advanced tutorials with complete instructions for creating fun forms such as a Pikachu, a snake, and a dragon (that took 72 hours to make!). During the COVID-19 pandemic, Yonatan added several new artistic approaches to his repertoire, reflecting modern and more abstract styles.